Ordinary, Extraordinary Jane Austen

The Story of Six Novels, Three Notebooks, a Writing Box, and One Clever Girl

By Deborah Hopkinson   Illustrations by Qin Leng

BALZER + BRAY
An Imprint of HarperCollinsPublishers

Balzer + Bray is an imprint of HarperCollins Publishers.

Ordinary, Extraordinary Jane Austen
Text copyright © 2018 by Deborah Hopkinson
Illustrations copyright © 2018 by Qin Leng
All rights reserved. Manufactured in China.
No part of this book may be used or reproduced in any manner whatsoever without written permission except
in the case of brief quotations embodied in critical articles and reviews. For information address HarperCollins
Children's Books, a division of HarperCollins Publishers, 195 Broadway, New York, NY 10007.
www.harpercollinschildrens.com

Library of Congress Control Number: 2017938680
ISBN 978-0-06-237330-4

The artist used ink and watercolor on paper to create the illustrations for this book.
Typography by Dana Fritts
19 20 21 SCP 10 9 8 7 6 5 4 3 2

First Edition

"For what do we live,
but to make sport for our neighbors,
and laugh at them in our turn?"

—Jane Austen, *Pride and Prejudice*

It is a truth universally acknowledged
that Jane Austen is one of our greatest writers.
But it might surprise you to know that
Jane lived a simple life.
She wasn't rich
or even very famous in her time.

In fact, if you'd met Jane when she was a girl,
you might not have noticed her at all.
She was sometimes awkward
and a little shy,
especially when company arrived.

But even then,
clever Jane was always
watching and listening,
and smiling to herself
at the foolish things
people sometimes did and said.

Jane had plenty of people to observe
right in her own home.
Jane and her sister, Cassandra, were the only girls in a house
bursting with six boisterous brothers,
plus packs of boys who came to live
and study at their father's boarding school.
It was like growing up inside a story
full of fascinating (and noisy) characters.

Families back then made their own fun,
and the Austens were never bored.
They played word games,
cards, and charades.
Jane was especially good at
shuttlecock and cup and ball.

Of course, everybody loved to dance.
And in the evenings, the children listened (mostly)
while their father read aloud.

Each December, Jane's family
turned their old barn into a theater
staging well-known dramas
and comedies (Jane's favorites)
to entertain their friends and neighbors.

Jane loved painting sets,
creating costumes,
and making stories come to life.

There were plenty of stories for her to read, too.
Her father's great library boasted five hundred books
(almost all of them by men).
Since Jane had little outside schooling,
the library was her classroom.
And while Jane devoured everything,
from history to poetry to biographies,
she loved novels best of all.

Even as a young girl,
Jane was a reader
who knew exactly what she liked,
and precisely what she didn't.
So it's no surprise that when Jane was twelve
she began to scribble her own keen observations
and sharp, wry comments into the margins of books.

Jane had such fun writing
she began to pen little plays and stories
to make her family laugh out loud.
And when her older brothers went away
to college and the sea,
Jane sent witty letters
to keep them smiling far from home.

Jane's father believed in her talent.
He bought her three special notebooks
and, later, a fine mahogany writing box
so Jane could carry her work wherever she went.

While their brothers journeyed far
to make their mark in the world,
Jane and Cassandra stayed home.

Like other young ladies,
they played cards and danced,
shopped for lace to trim a bonnet,
and gossiped about suitors and marriage.
(Sometimes Jane even fell a little bit in love herself.)

All the while,
Jane kept reading and listening
and, of course, practicing her writing.
And when she was still just a teen,
Jane felt ready to write novels of her own.

Now, the most popular novels in Jane's time
were adventures and romances,
with gallant heroes
rescuing fair, fainting heroines
from dark, gloomy castles
and (of course!)
despicable, dangerous villains.

But Jane wanted *her* books
to hold up a mirror to the ordinary world
so readers could recognize (and laugh at) themselves.

So Jane went her own way,
inventing a new kind of story
about real people, and sisters (like Cassandra and herself),
who longed to follow their dreams.

And that is exactly what she did.
By the time she was twenty-one,
Jane had written three novels.
Jane's proud father sent one to a publisher,
which, alas, turned it down.

But Jane was a writer who didn't give up.
Like an artist using a fine brush,
Jane kept working to make her stories
better and better,
until each word was perfect.

At long last, another publisher said yes!

During her lifetime,
four of Jane's six major novels were published
without her real name,
which was sometimes the custom then.
(The title page simply read "by a lady.")

But everyone was curious to know
who this talented lady was,
and Jane's secret soon leaked out.

Jane didn't mind.
She rather liked being known as an author.

And so, although Jane died
when she was only forty-one,
she lived long enough to achieve her dream.

Now, two hundred years later,
I wonder if Jane would be surprised to learn
that her books are still read and loved

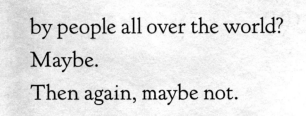

by people all over the world?
Maybe.
Then again, maybe not.

For perhaps there was a moment
when young Jane stood alone in
her father's grand library,
with the works of great men all around her,
and said to herself, "I can do this.

I can do even better.
I will write about the ordinary world
in the most extraordinary way."

That, dear reader, is exactly what she did.

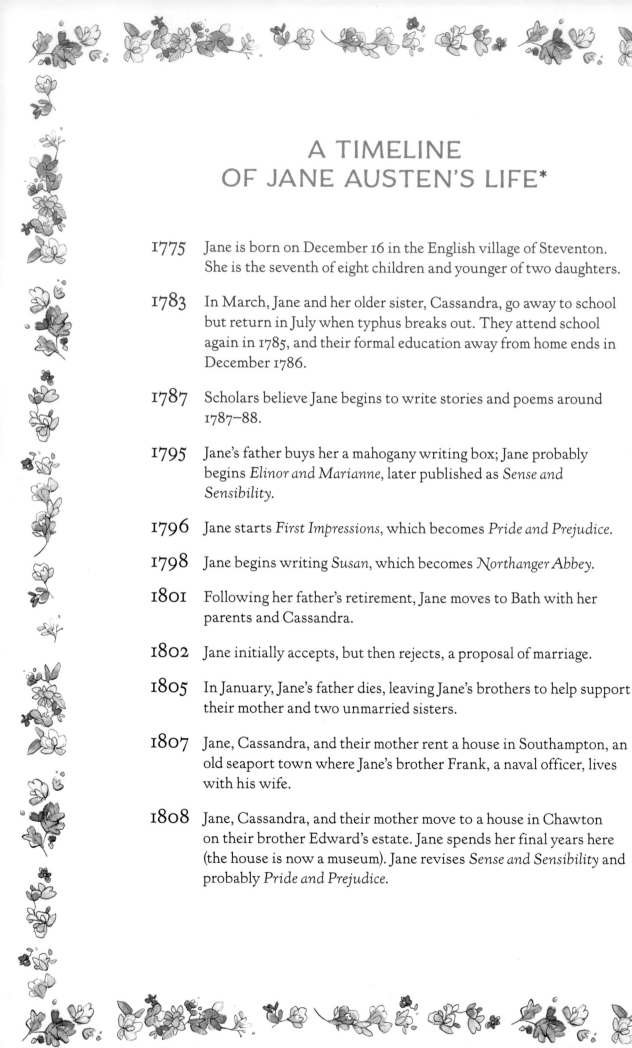

A TIMELINE
OF JANE AUSTEN'S LIFE*

1775   Jane is born on December 16 in the English village of Steventon. She is the seventh of eight children and younger of two daughters.

1783   In March, Jane and her older sister, Cassandra, go away to school but return in July when typhus breaks out. They attend school again in 1785, and their formal education away from home ends in December 1786.

1787   Scholars believe Jane begins to write stories and poems around 1787–88.

1795   Jane's father buys her a mahogany writing box; Jane probably begins *Elinor and Marianne*, later published as *Sense and Sensibility*.

1796   Jane starts *First Impressions*, which becomes *Pride and Prejudice*.

1798   Jane begins writing *Susan*, which becomes *Northanger Abbey*.

1801   Following her father's retirement, Jane moves to Bath with her parents and Cassandra.

1802   Jane initially accepts, but then rejects, a proposal of marriage.

1805   In January, Jane's father dies, leaving Jane's brothers to help support their mother and two unmarried sisters.

1807   Jane, Cassandra, and their mother rent a house in Southampton, an old seaport town where Jane's brother Frank, a naval officer, lives with his wife.

1808   Jane, Cassandra, and their mother move to a house in Chawton on their brother Edward's estate. Jane spends her final years here (the house is now a museum). Jane revises *Sense and Sensibility* and probably *Pride and Prejudice*.

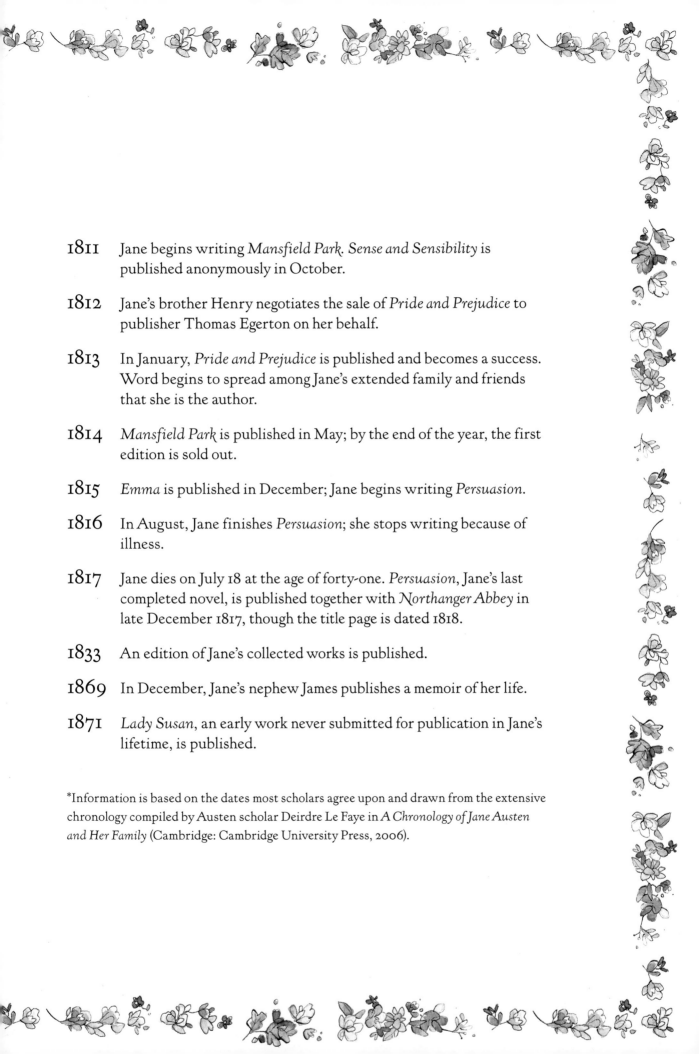

1811 Jane begins writing *Mansfield Park*. *Sense and Sensibility* is published anonymously in October.

1812 Jane's brother Henry negotiates the sale of *Pride and Prejudice* to publisher Thomas Egerton on her behalf.

1813 In January, *Pride and Prejudice* is published and becomes a success. Word begins to spread among Jane's extended family and friends that she is the author.

1814 *Mansfield Park* is published in May; by the end of the year, the first edition is sold out.

1815 *Emma* is published in December; Jane begins writing *Persuasion*.

1816 In August, Jane finishes *Persuasion*; she stops writing because of illness.

1817 Jane dies on July 18 at the age of forty-one. *Persuasion*, Jane's last completed novel, is published together with *Northanger Abbey* in late December 1817, though the title page is dated 1818.

1833 An edition of Jane's collected works is published.

1869 In December, Jane's nephew James publishes a memoir of her life.

1871 *Lady Susan*, an early work never submitted for publication in Jane's lifetime, is published.

*Information is based on the dates most scholars agree upon and drawn from the extensive chronology compiled by Austen scholar Deirdre Le Faye in *A Chronology of Jane Austen and Her Family* (Cambridge: Cambridge University Press, 2006).

JANE'S BOOKSHELF

Sense and Sensibility

PUBLISHED: 1811

FAMOUS QUOTES:

" . . . the more I know of the world, the more I am convinced
that I shall never see a man whom I can really love."

"Seven years would be insufficient to make
some people acquainted with each other, and seven days
are more than enough for others."

WHAT IT'S ABOUT:

Two sisters, Elinor and Marianne Dashwood, along with
their mother and younger sister, are turned out of the family
home after their father's death. Elinor and Marianne each face
obstacles on the path to finding true love.

Pride and Prejudice

PUBLISHED: 1813

FAMOUS QUOTES:

"It is a truth universally acknowledged, that a single man in
possession of a good fortune, must be in want of a wife."

"For what do we live, but to make sport for our neighbors,
and laugh at them in our turn?"

WHAT IT'S ABOUT:

When a handsome and rich young man moves into the
neighborhood, Mrs. Bennet, the mother of five daughters,
begins matchmaking. Jane Austen's most popular novel has
inspired film adaptations, parodies, and sequels.

Mansfield Park

PUBLISHED: 1814

FAMOUS QUOTES:

"Nothing ever fatigues me but doing what I do not like."

"We have all a better guide in ourselves, if we would
attend to it, than any other person can be."

WHAT IT'S ABOUT:

A poor girl named Fanny Price goes to live with her
wealthy aunt and uncle and their four children. Modest and
conscientious, Fanny falls in love with Edmund, the younger son,
and must watch as he flirts with the sophisticated
(but shallow) Mary Crawford.

Emma

PUBLISHED: 1815

FAMOUS QUOTES:

"The real evils, indeed, of Emma's situation were
the power of having rather too much her own way,
and a disposition to think a little too well of herself. . . . ."

"If I loved you less, I might be able to talk about it more."

WHAT IT'S ABOUT:

The young and beautiful Emma Woodhouse loves
matchmaking, but her efforts lead to one disaster after
another. Meanwhile, what about Emma's own heart?

Northanger Abbey

PUBLISHED: 1817

FAMOUS QUOTES:
"No one who had ever seen Catherine Morland in her infancy would have supposed her born to be a heroine."

"She was fond of all boys' plays, and greatly preferred cricket not merely to dolls, but to the more heroic enjoyments of infancy, nursing a dormouse, feeding a canary-bird, or watering a rose-bush."

WHAT IT'S ABOUT:
In the bustling city of Bath, Catherine Morland meets new and exciting acquaintances. She accepts an invitation to visit Henry Tilney and his family at Northanger Abbey. Are there mysteries hidden in the old house, or is Catherine, who loves reading Gothic novels and romances, simply imagining things?

Persuasion

PUBLISHED: 1817

FAMOUS QUOTES:
"We certainly do not forget you, so soon as you forget us. . . . We live at home, quiet, confined, and our feelings prey upon us."

"Men have had every advantage of us in telling their own story. Education has been theirs in so much higher a degree; the pen has been in their hands."

WHAT IT'S ABOUT:
Eight years before, Anne Elliot was persuaded to refuse an offer of marriage. When her past suitor, Captain Frederick Wentworth, returns looking for a bride he is considered quite a catch by girls younger and prettier than Anne. Will he even look at Anne again, never mind forgive her for what happened?

Learn more about Jane on the Internet

Jane Austen's House Museum
Take a peek at Jane's Chawton house.
www.jane-austens-house-museum.org.uk

Jane Austen Society of the United Kingdom
Online exhibits include pictures of the clothes Jane would have worn,
as well as information on Jane's novels.
www.janeaustensoci.freeuk.com

Jane Austen Society of North America
Jane still has fan clubs all over the world!
There's even an essay contest for students in high school or above.
www.jasna.org

Jane Austen at the British Library
See Cassandra's portrait of Jane and images from Jane's books.
Jane Austen's portable writing desk is at the British Library, too.
www.bl.uk/people/jane-austen

History of Jane's Portable Mahogany Writing Desk
www.jasna.org/persuasions/printed/number30/welland.pdf

Books

There are many editions and adaptations of Jane's own books available, as well as
works about Jane herself. Here are a few resources I used in my research:

Byrne, Paula. *The Real Jane Austen: A Life in Small Things*. New York: Harper, 2013.

Halperin, John. *The Life of Jane Austen*. Baltimore: Johns Hopkins University Press, 1984.

Honan, Park. *Jane Austen: Her Life*. New York: Ballentine Books, 1989.

Le Faye, Deirdre. *A Chronology of Jane Austen and Her Family*. Cambridge: Cambridge
University Press, 2006.

———, ed. *Jane Austen's Letters*. Oxford: Oxford University Press, 2011.

With love to my grandson,
Oliver Sawyer, may you grow up
to treasure books just like
Jane Austen

—D.H.

To all book lovers

—Q.L.